Dear Reader,

You are about to find out about a giant place called the World which is where I live.

In this book I have tried to explain about some of the best things in the World like...

* Boyfriends and Girlfriends
* How to Make People Fancy You
* Booze
* Scrumptious Nosh
* Pants

...and about some of the nasty things like...

* Scratchy Lav Paper
* Exploding Goolies
* Cold Bogey Curry
* Hairy Bits in the Bath

If I have left anything out I'm sorry but it's a very big place.

love from
Purple Ronnie
X X X

The Beginning of Time

Imagine a place where there were no burgers or beer or hot dogs

Imagine a place without chips or chocolate or chocolate chips or ketchup or anything

Imagine a place where there's nothing to natter about and no-one to cuddle up with

Imagine a place where nothing's ever on T.V. and there's no T.V. not to watch it on

Imagine a place where it's night all the time, where it's cold and dark and lonely

That's what it was like in the beginning of time when the only person around was GOD

Before The World was Invented
∾ by Purple Ronnie ∾

Not surprisingly God didn't think it was much fun. He was bored and lonely and sometimes quite scared

And because it was dark he quite often bumped into things

When God went to bed he used to shut his eyes and dream for hours about inventing this place that he could muck around and have fun in

There would be all sorts of smells and feelings and tastes in this place and every day there would be friends to explore new things with

He wanted something like a gigantic bouncy castle with flowers and trees and monkeys and butterflies and streams and mountains and stuff like that

Then all of a sudden God had a brilliant idea. He saved up loads of his most powerful magic and mixed it up with his biggest wishes then he sprinkled on top his most powerful spell in history EVER

That night God didn't have any dreams at all and when he looked out of the window the next day he felt smashing

Dangling from the roof of the sky was a sort of gigantic round pudding

All the grooviest treats and surprises he'd ever wanted were stuffed inside that pudding. what's more he was the king of it

yippee!

swing

HO HO HO

For the first time in his life God laughed...

...He had invented THE WORLD

Names for new invention
- THE PUDDING X
- SUPERLAND ?
- THE WORLD ✓
- NORMAN SNACKELFIZZER X
  ↑ too muddly

?

The First People

The first people were Adam and Eve. They lived in the world when it was almost brand new. The trouble is they couldn't find any instructions to go with it

Because of this they quite often got in a muddle about how to work all the new things and what it was like to be people

First of all they went around completely bare

When they felt hungry they didn't know what to eat or how to get it into their tummies

And when they felt saucy they had to try millions of experiments before they got it right

Adam and Eve thought that Doing It was one of the best inventions ever, so they had millions of babies who all found girlfriends or boyfriends and had millions more babies

In the end all the different places in the world became full of people. Most of them were friendly and polite but some of them are still very naughty

Because of this God had to make a list of important instructions which people must <u>never</u> forget

These are the main ones...

INSTRUCTIONS FOR LIVING

1. Thou shalt not have rude thoughts about thy mate's girlfriend

2. Thou art not allowed Ketchup _and_ mustard with thy sausages

3. Thou shalt not leave hairy bits in the bath

4. If thy enemy bashes thee in thou shalt ask him to bog off politely

5. Thou shalt always say thy girlfriend looks fantastic when she dresses up

6. Thou shalt not point at baldies

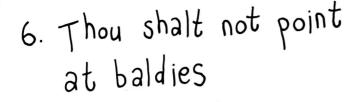

7. If thou eatest not thy meat thou canst not have any pudding

8. Thou shalt not waft thy bottom burps towards other people and pretend that thou was not the maker of the bottom burp in the first place

9. Thou shalt not try to escape the washing up

10. Thou shalt not squash thy girlfriend out of the bed, nor shalt thou hog the blankets

What Happens in Hell

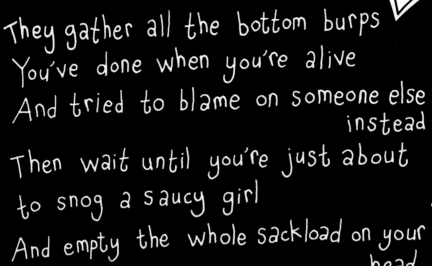

They gather all the bottom burps
You've done when you're alive
And tried to blame on someone else
instead
Then wait until you're just about
to snog a saucy girl
And empty the whole sackload on your
head

They wire up your privates
Then they dip you in ice cream
And ask a hundred girls to have a scoff
But if you move a muscle
Or your doodah starts to grow
The wires touch and blow your goolies off

They've got a giant movie screen
On which they show your life
And blare out all the secrets that
you have
Then they pause and show slow motions
of the stupid things you've done
With action replays of you on the lav

Drinking is one of the main things that keeps us alive. If we didn't drink we'd go all dry and crumbly like biscuits and people would have to sweep us up off the floor.

The main drink is water which you can tell by 3 things

1 | It's completely see-through

2 | It doesn't taste of anything

Well...um... it's sort of ...quite...kind of... just wet

3 | You don't feel any nicer after you've had some

Because water is so boring lots of people got together and tried millions of experiments to invent other sorts of drinks

Some people took off their shoes and stamped on huge piles of grapes

squish

hic

Some people tried to make tasty recipes with plants and flowers

And some people just squeezed out their mouldy vegetables

whiff

The one thing they all came up with was BOOZE

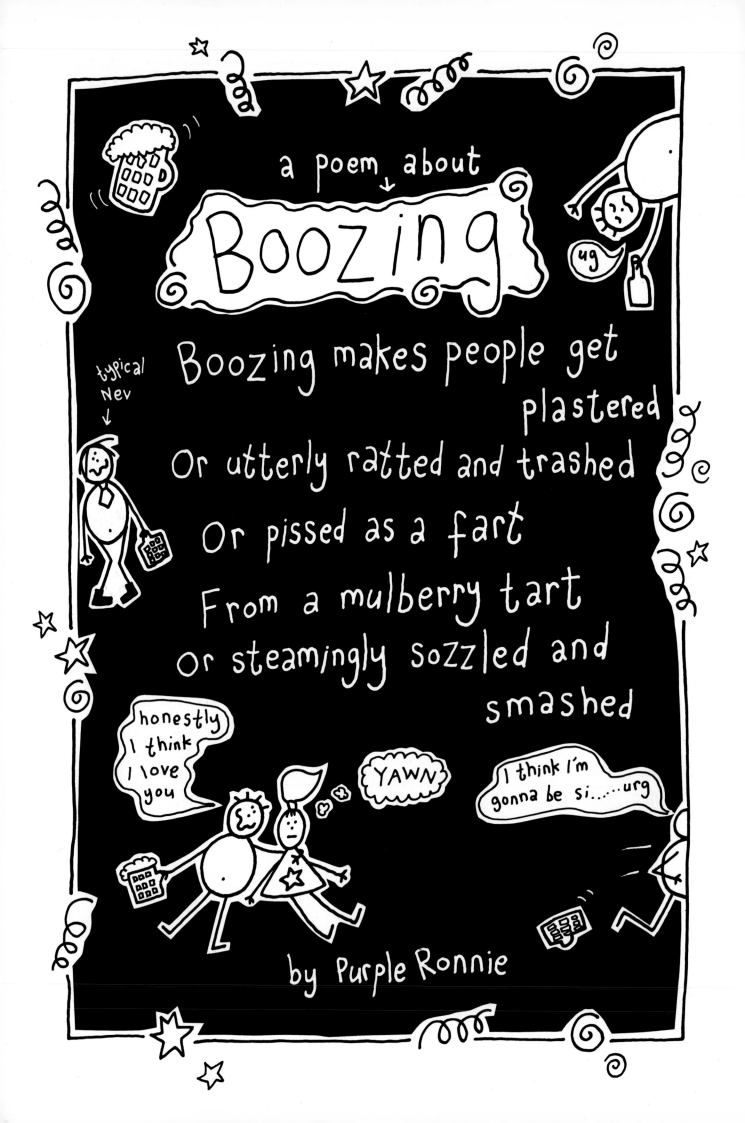

The Difference That Booze Makes

Drinking Chart

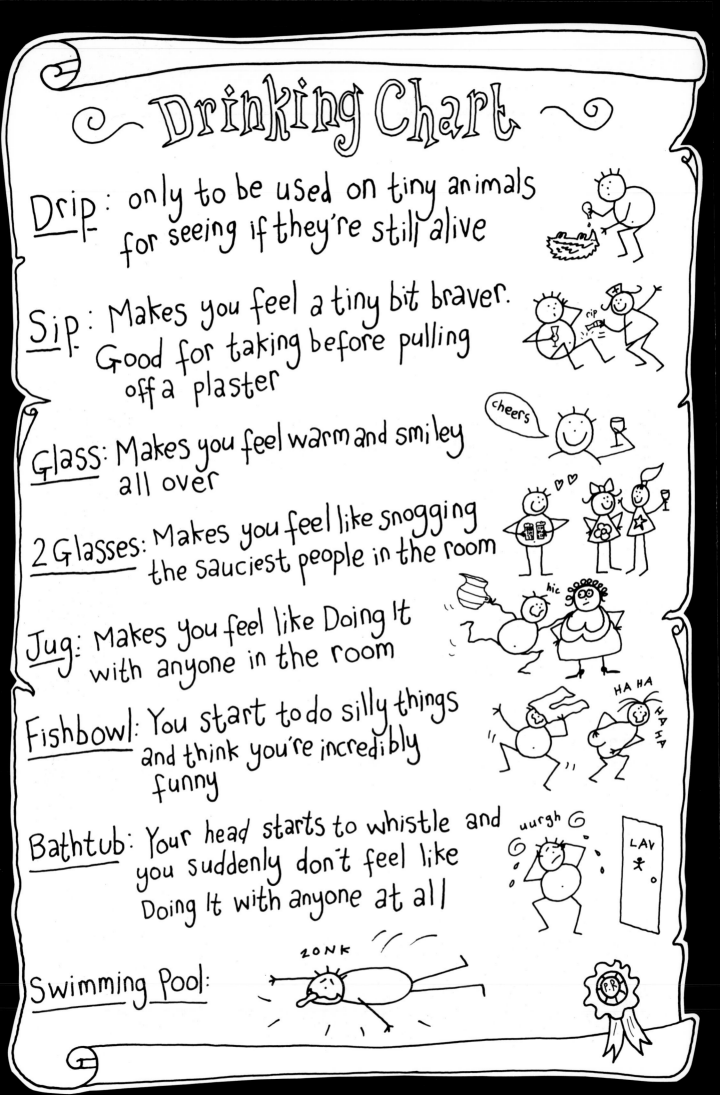

Drip: only to be used on tiny animals for seeing if they're still alive

Sip: Makes you feel a tiny bit braver. Good for taking before pulling off a plaster

Glass: Makes you feel warm and smiley all over

2 Glasses: Makes you feel like snogging the sauciest people in the room

Jug: Makes you feel like Doing It with anyone in the room

Fishbowl: You start to do silly things and think you're incredibly funny

Bathtub: Your head starts to whistle and you suddenly don't feel like Doing It with anyone at all

Swimming Pool:

The Dog and Purple Cocktail Menu

PURPLE BREW

Made in my bedroom

Good Things: Cheap, masses of it

Not so Good Things: Tastes horrid, makes you go to the lav for ages

Purpo Brewo de Mexico

Costs twice as much as normal beer and comes in tiny bottles. Tastes like wee. Only to be used for being trendy

Double Trouser Wobbling Whoopee Scorcher Super Snogger

Great for asking girls if they want one. Creamy and sticky with all sorts of gadgets in it

a poem about my Homebrew

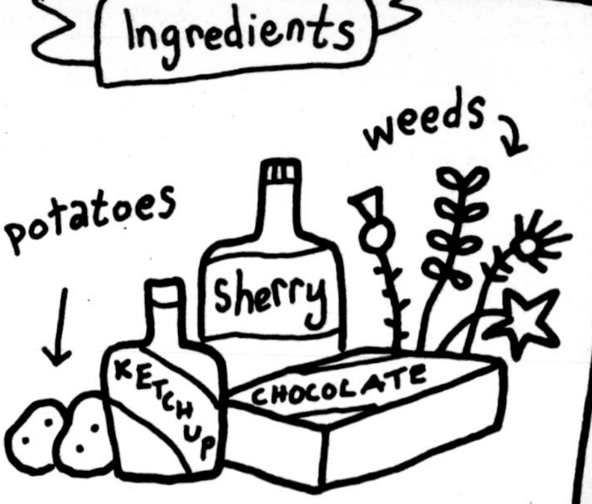

Me and my mates drank some homebrew

I made in my bedroom last year

My brain went all swirly

Poor Gordon went curly

And Neville came over all queer

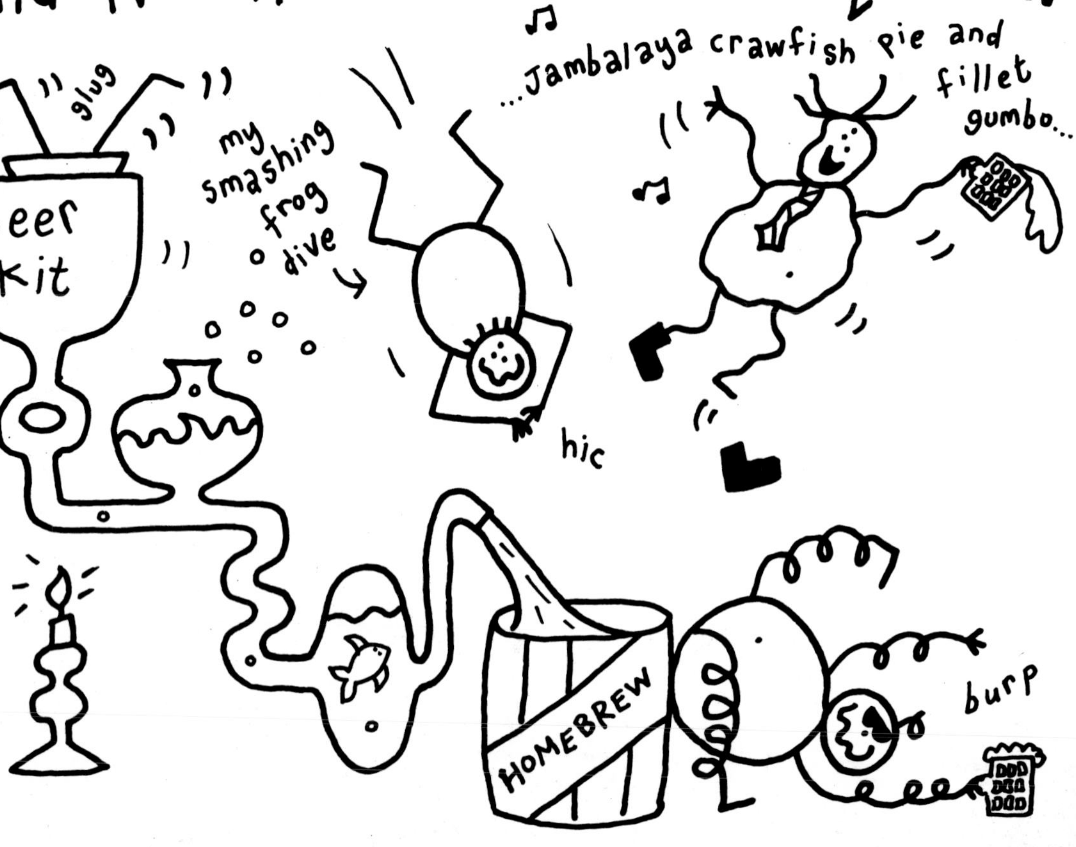

by Purple Ronnie

a poem about

lager louts

phew

double vindaloo botty burner special

Lager louts love going out with
the lads
In fact it's their favourite trick
To gobble down masses of curry and
beer

And pass out in piles of sick

CURRY PALACE

Spicy waft

get your boobies out for the lads...
...Ooof

BUS STOP

burp

sick puddle

FLURB

hic

crunch

by Purple Ronnie

The History of
Private Parts

Ages ago when people first started speaking they found the cleverest man in the world and they gave him the job of thinking up good words and names for everything he could see

Because everyone went around bare the first thing he saw was men's parts. These were easy to think up loads of names for because they behaved in all sorts of funny ways

But when his girlfriend asked him to think up a good name for her parts he suddenly realized that he had used up all his part words and he didn't have any left

He spent ages trying to come up with a good word but he found it very difficult because his girl's parts didn't dangle around like his. In the end he died of brainache

Ever since then the brainiest people from all over the world have tried to think up a good word

But to this day a girl's parts are the one thing left in the whole world that still doesn't have a proper name

a poem about

Wibbly-Wobbly Bits

Some people say they're called
bosoms
Others just say they're called tits
But the words I like best
For describing your chest
Are your <u>wibbly</u>-<u>wobbly</u> bits

...mmmm wibbly wobbly bits

by
Purple
Ronnie

Purple Ronnie's Guide to PANTS

Pant Fact 1

Pants were the first invention ever in the whole world. The first pants were made of leaves and bits of string

Leaf pants were not very good because:

1 They went brown and mouldy too quickly

2 Everyone could tell when you were doing a bottom burp

Pant Fact 2

In the Olden Days Knights in armour invented spiky metal pants for their girlfriends to wear

These were abolished when men started wanting to wear girls' undies

Pant Fact 3

Make-you-look-like-you've-got-a-giant-Doodah Pants were invented by Shakespeare

These are still worn by Pop Stars and Neville

Pant Styles

Granny Pants

Granny Pants stretch from just under your armpits to just above your feet. They are made from thick baggy sacks and are covered in frills. Granny pants always smell of poison

Sports Pants

Sports pants are for squeezing men's bits into the smallest shape possible. Only to be worn for short periods of time or your privates might melt

French Pants

French pants are for looking sexy in. They are so slippery that if you aren't careful you can slide off your chair and collapse on the floor

Squashing Pants

Squashing pants squish your tummy and bottom together to make you look thinner When you wear squashing pants steam comes out of your ears, you walk in a funny way and sometimes bits of tummy squish out over the edge

String Pants

No-one knows why string pants were invented. Do not wear them infront of girls. String pants are good for straining homemade beer and catching fish

G-String Pants

G-String Pants are like tying a tiny hanky round your parts. Do not wear G-string pants if you have a flabby bottom Cos you might not find them again for ages

a poem for a BOYFRIEND

You're a hunky handsome heart-throb
You're a fab and groovy dude
You're a juicy lump of gorgeousness
A scrumptious plate of food
You're a hot and horny lover
And if I had my way
I would smother you in chocolate
And feast on you all day

by Purple Ronnie

sizzle yipee

CHOC SPREAD

Boyfriends and Girlfriends

In the Olden Days when you were choosing boyfriends and girlfriends people thought the best thing was to have piles of cash and be incredibly nobby...

... but nowadays people think the most important thing is what you look like!!/

How to Look Fantastic for Love

STEP 1: Take off all your clothes and sit in a boiling hot room

STEP 2: Rubbing, Ripping, Tweaking and Squeezing

STEP 3: Mix up stuff from nature to make yourself fresh and clean

STEP 4: Take plenty of exercise

STEP 5: Give Yourself a treat once in a while

STEP 6: What you can't change by nature...Doctor Swindle will change for money

a poem about dieting

I think I might go on a diet
All of my friends say it's great
I like the bit where you sneak
down the stairs
And pile loads of grub on your
plate

by Purple Ronnie

The Ways Boys and Girls Think

BOYS

Boys' brains are like great big meat pies with lots of jelly and gristle inside and their heads are made of cement

chewy fat and gristly bits

thick crust

rock hard ↑

This means it is difficult to get new thoughts into a boy's head

let's go to the seaside
why don't we have a romantic walk?
I want to go shopping
Who wants to go to the fun fair?
can we go to the disco?

I know let's get pissed and watch football

GIRLS

Girls' brains are more like huge fluffy clouds. Sometimes this means that incredibly complicated thoughts can shoot around in them like lightning ...

If Purple and Gordon are friends and Neville fancies Shirlee and Purple loves Maisy but Gordon is Shirlee's best mate then that means Gordon definitely fancies ME!

... sometimes that air and space is the only thing in there

... and sometimes that there are terrible thunderstorms when the only thing to do is run for it

Boys are easier to understand because their brains are wired straight to their privates so they mostly only think of one thing

But girls brains are more complicated and can think about lots of things at the same time

a poem about

Men I Like

I like men who talk
About interesting things
Like music and science and art,
But most men I know
When they've had a few drinks
Just talk about sex and then
fart

by Purple
Ronnie

a poem about **floozies**

They love to go shopping together
And spend all the money they have
At night they just dance round
their handbags

And laugh about boys in the lav

by Purple Ronnie

The differences between Hunks and Weeds

Boyfriends come in 2 styles:-

HUNKS: who are macho and bossy and tell you what to do all the time

AND

WEEDS: who are dreamy and funny and don't even know what to do themselves

Here is how to tell the difference:-

Girls think hunks are tough

Weeds think girls are tough

Hunks make a rumpus

Weeds make a fuss

a poem for a

Lover

If someone invented a gadget
That made me terrific in bed
I think I'd buy twenty-five
                thousand
And do it with you till I'm
                dead

by Purple Ronnie

a poem about Macho Men

Some men think it's cool to bare

A bulging chest with loads of hair

But if you talk to one you'll find

His brains are stuck up his behind

by Purple Ronnie

How to Be a Boyfriend

Sometimes you've got to be macho
And do lots of things that are tough
But sometimes it's best to be quiet and gentle
And say loads of soppy type stuff

It's good to have hundreds of muscles
And girls always like a nice bum
But you mustn't be hairy or sweaty or fat
Or have any flab on your tum

Don't ever talk about football
Or make nasty smells in the bed
Or joke about bosoms with mates in the pub
Or drink till you're out of your head

You've got to be funny and clever
And do loads of things by surprise
Like shouting out loud in the back
                    of the bus
"My girlfriend's got beautiful eyes!"

You don't need to have too much money
But make sure you've just got enough
To buy loads of presents and chocolates
                    and flowers
And sexy silk undies and stuff

Say to your girlfriend "you're gorgeous
Your body's a twelve out of ten
You're sexy and beautiful, clever and kind"
Then tell her all over again

Blah Blah Blah

what a super boyfriend

a poem about a
↓
Cuddle Token

I've got you something
wonderful
That can't be smashed
or broken
I hope you use it lots
Cos it's my special cuddle
token

my
special
present
↓

Cuddle
CUDDLE
BOX

by
Purple
Ronnie

How to Live For Ever

Neville went off to find out the mysterious secret of how to live for ever.

Across many deep oceans and dry deserts he travelled until he was totally fagged out

At last Nev reached a giant tree beside a dark cave in which was sitting the Wisest Man in the World and these are the secrets he told him :—

If you want to live for ever
You must sleep inside a tree

And every time you're thirsty
You should drink a pint of wee

Ask a load of sexy girls
To stroke you every day

And don't do any work at all
just muck around and play

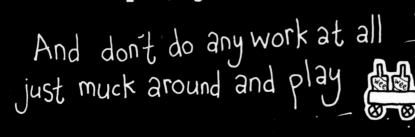

Grow a wild hairy beard
That stretches to your tummy

And find a lot of lovely fans
who give you loads of money

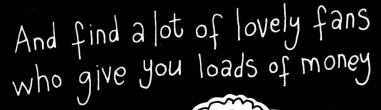

Meditate for hours on
the things that you like best

And get a string of funny stones
to dangle from your chest

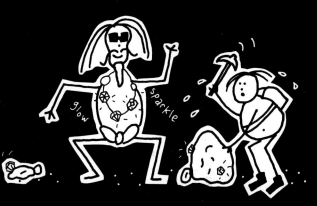

Eat beetles for your breakfast
with a pinch of powdered flea

And that's how to live for ever Nev
-Now have some slug slime tea

It is no use fibbing about
what you have done because
God's mates are the judges
and they are very clever
☆

But if you have been friendly and given all
your sweets to old ladies and helped poorly animals
then you can go whizzing up to Heaven and have
a smashing time for ever and ever

Special Tip ☆

If you have got any money
left when you have your
chat with God you will not
be allowed into Heaven
so it's best to spend
it all first

The End of the World

I hope that I'm there at the End of the World
When everyone stands in a queue
And says all the wickedest things that they've done
And the bad things they've wanted to do

Naughty folk's heads will cave in and explode
And goo will spurt out of their brains
Their tummies will tangle and turn inside out
And their bottoms will burst into flames

But people like me who've been lovely and kind
Will rocket straight up to the sky
And watch the whole rumpus from big squashy beds
With loads of free ale and fudge pie

And angels will cuddle and stroke us
And say how fantastic we are
And how out of all of the people they've met
We're the smashingly coolest by far